# PUA NANI

# PUA NANI

*Photographed by Douglas Peebles*

*Written by Jeri Bostwick*
*Designed by Momi Cazimero*

MUTUAL PUBLISHING OF HONOLULU

*The publishers would like to thank*
*the following corporate sponsors*
*for their help with* **Pua Nani.**

*Hawaiian Air*

*Light Inc.*

*Fuji Photo Film of Hawaii Inc.*

*We would also like to give our thanks*
*to each of the Gardens represented*
*and especially to Paul Weissich,*
*Bob Leinau, Keith Woolliams, Greg Koob,*
*Marc Code, Judy Sanehira, Nancy Quinn,*
*Bob Hirano, Howard Cooper, Carl Lindquist,*
*Lawrence Tachibana, Steve Siegfried, Riki Saito,*
*Scott Lucas, Warren McCord and Dr. Philip Parvin.*

*Photographs © 1987 by Douglas Peebles*
*Copyright © 1987 by Mutual Publishing*
*2055 N. King St.*
*Honolulu, Hawaii 96819*
*(808) 924-7732*

*Printed in Japan*

# HAWAII,
# ISLANDS
# OF
# GARDENS

*WHERE DREAMS GO THAT WANT TO COME TRUE*

The Hawaiian Islands came boiling out of the earth's core, each in its own time, from the Pacific Ocean "hot spot" still adding lava shores to the Big Island of Hawaii.

As the Pacific tectonic plate pushed the islands northwest with inexorable movement, they were barren gray-brown mountains of lava, towering 30,000 feet from the ocean bottom.

Flowers and trees, so much a part of the islands today, arrived slowly. Some came on the wings of trade winds, as did spores of the many ferns or, as the coconut, floated on the crest of the ocean; some were carried by birds on their feathers or rode with man on canoes, frigates, steamships and planes.

Each had crossed nearly 2,000 miles of ocean to produce the lush mountains and valleys, where a practiced eye can count 43 shades of green on a sunny day.

Hawaii's first arrivals were delicate—feathery **lehua;** lacy coral hibiscus; tiny rain lilies; brilliant **hau** that changes from yellow in the morning to red at sunset; small white flowers of **ipu;** bright orange **kou;** and dainty pink field orchids.

Showy exotic travelers, quite at home in Hawaii, are the flaming torch ginger; brilliant red, pink and orange anthuriums; radiant, ruffled, purple and lavender orchids; fluorescent heliconia; and orange bird-of-paradise, poised for flight. Plus the perfumed, luminescent whites—plumeria, **pikake,** tiare tahiti, stephanotis and ginger.

Throughout the years they have all become unmistakably Hawaii's **pua nani**—beautiful flowers.

This semi-tropical, seasonless land is ever blooming, and the flowers mark a circling year.

Hedges of poinsettias herald the Christmas season; cup of gold arrives with the New Year; royal poinciana and shower trees bloom in May and June; night-blooming cereus perfumes August; foamy white porana and orange colvillea appear in October. Bougainvillea, hibiscus, orchids and oleander bloom year-round.

Flowers are part of Hawaii's daily life. Women wear flowers in their hair as they shop and wreathe friends with fragrant leis; statues wear garlands on holidays or carry nosegays; and parade horses are blanketed in blossoms.

Flowers are part of great moments. Who can ever forget the great silversword gleaming in an early sunrise at the 10,000-foot caldera of Maui's Haleakala, like some elegant alien being from another world? Or the brilliance of massed poinsettia glowing beside white roses along the Big Island's Captain Cook Highway in December? Or who can forget Oahu's streets, a pastel portrait of spring in pink, peach and yellow shower trees? Or Kauai's Kokee Park, where, in winter, Glory bushes purple the hills and Christmas berry flaunts its seasonal scarlet? Or that every house on each island has flowering baskets hanging from porch and eaves and a riot of bloom in the front yard?

**Pua Nani** is a journey through Kauai, Oahu, Maui and Hawaii to visit their fragrant green valleys and rainbow gardens through the magic of Douglas Peebles' camera lens.

With the Western world's discovery of the Hawaiian Islands came towns, roadways, developments, and a gradual shrinking of wilderness vistas. Then, throughout the islands, people set aside special areas to preserve the beauty and uniqueness of Hawaii in special parks and gardens.

**Pua Nani** visits the loveliest on each island.

But, like a home garden, this book's photographs are not programmed by botanic genus, but are served as the Hawaiian favorite—a "mixed plate" of all that is lovely, not only in structured botanic gardens, but in the rainbow profusion of Hawaii's front yards.

Indeed, all Hawaii is a garden.

*Napali Coast*

# GARDENS OF KAUAI

*Aina Kihapai Poina Ole*
*A GARDENLAND ONE NEVER FORGETS*

*Kauai, northernmost of the main Hawaiian Islands, is about 5.5 million years old and has weathered over those years into a land of rich red soil and inviting white sand beaches.*

*This nearly round island has, also, the only true rivers of any Hawaiian island. The mountain-creator, Mt. Waialeale, (mother-of-waters) lifts her 5,000-foot truncated head directly into the path of the constant trade winds, extracting 448 inches of rain annually from the moisture-laden clouds.*

*From the changeless mist over the caldera's Alakai Swamp, which centers the island, come a hundred dancing, rippling streamlets, growing into hundreds of sparkling waterfalls that spill into ravines and canyons to form five major rivers.*

*Kauai's singing waters and the springtime consistency of the world's greatest climate may just be the reasons this special island is the greenest, most flower adorned of all the Hawaiian islands, and is lovingly known as the Garden Isle.*

*Kauai has been around longer. It was the first discovered and settled by the Marquesan Polynesian voyagers around A.D. 200–500, has been cultivated longer, and has had more time to garner migrant seeds and plants.*

*Several of the state's most special and unusual public gardens flourish here in unforgettable beauty.*

*The history of Pacific Tropical Botanical Gardens, the only private educational gardens chartered by Congress, is long and varied.*

*Its home, Lawai, has been a fruitful and beautiful valley for centuries. Early Hawaiians grew taro here; the Chinese later cultivated rice in the same lava terraces; still later — even today — sugar cane grows in the upper reaches.*

*Nature created its immutable landscape on the sunny south shore of the island. The wide blue bay caresses a crescent-shaped white sand beach backed by a long sweep of palm-studded flatland. The lower valley is bordered by lava cliffs draped in magenta bougainvillea.*

*The first gardener who planted "just for pleasure" in this enchanted place was Queen Emma, wife of King Kamehameha IV. She is said to have set out the bougainvillea herself and planned an extensive garden dedicated to flowers, in the 1870s. A Queen Emma orchid still grows in the Pacific Tropical Botanical Gardens.*

*At her death the garden retreated to a wild state until rediscovered in 1937 by Robert Allerton and John Gregg Allerton, transplanted, millionaire Midwesterners, and talented amateur landscapists. The Queen's Garden was greatly expanded for the Allertons' Garden with lily pools, palatial gazebos and outstanding, carefully designed tropical plantings.*

*Now attached to the Allerton Gardens — or perhaps the other way around — the Pacific Tropical Botanical Gardens has been called "one of the most prestigious, attractive, and largely unknown gardens in the world." This sequestered "Garden of Eden" is a tropical plant research station created to save endangered plants, to locate and propagate plants of medicinal importance and make the findings "of public use."*

*The world-famous collections include the Rare and Endangered Plants Endemic to the Hawaiian Islands Collection, which is a new display garden planted almost exclusively in native Hawaiian plants. The Medicinal Plants Collection is encircled by high cliffs and with varied terrain, and is becoming one of the garden's most beautiful areas. The Erythrina Species and Hybrids (varieties of flowering trees, i.e., coral trees) is the largest collection in cultivation with more than 100 families represented from all over the world and with a number of new ornamental hybrids.*

*The Palm Collection is represented by nearly 600 families. There are more than 30 different varieties from the Pacific Basin where plant quarantine today prevents their import. At the Lawai Garden there is a planting of double coconuts, now an endangered species, from the Seychelle Islands. The Ethnobotanical Collections contain varieties of breadfruit, banana, taro and edible pandanus and support a gene bank of those plants rapidly being depleted in the Pacific.*

Visitors can admire colorful collections of orchids and gingers, bromeliads and erythrina, tropical ornamentals such as heliconia and bird of paradise, and even water lilies with leaves strong enough to support a man.

The Lawai stream wanders through the Pacific Tropical Botanical Garden and downhill through the Lawai Kai Allerton Gardens, sliding with sublime grace into a unique system of structured water courses.

The Allerton Gardens are a fantasy of rainbow colors and shades of green, punctuated by a collection of art and architectural whimseys—statuary, waterfalls, pools and fountains, arbors, bowers, colonnades, pergolas and gazebos. Many parts of the fascinating gardens are now available for public viewing with visits to the Pacific Botanical Garden. Tours of both gardens are by reservation only, Monday through Saturday. Call Pacific Tropical Botanical Garden on Kauai for information.

At the Plantation Gardens on Poipu Beach, the grounds have three freshwater ponds from the most ancient of Hawaiian days and present a pleasant vista and fertile soil for the "handpicked tropical plant specimens" Mr. and Mrs. Hector Moir brought back from their world travels. Hector Moir was manager of Kauai's first sugar plantation and made many business voyages throughout the tropics.

Their garden, often called "the cactus gardens," has twenty-foot spiny giants and branching succulents surrounded by the red torches of aloes, orchids, night-blooming cereus, and flowering tropical trees.

Bromeliads encircle ponds of water lilies, and delicate Singapore plumerias blossom next to huge saguaro cactus and spiny ocotillo. Here the red flame of the African poinsettia may grow to ten or fifteen feet.

The grounds, including ancient lava fireplaces, are preserved on their original sites. Artifacts of earlier days—a sugar mill wheel, whaling try-pots and ancient grindstones—are to be found at the turn of any path.

The Moir estate home has been converted into a restaurant called "Plantation Gardens." The gardens, photographs from the 1800s, and the graciousness of yesteryear are carefully maintained in welcoming guests and visitors.

A collection of over 4,000 native and introduced tropical and subtropical fruits, flowers and trees fills the twelve-and-a-half acres of Olu Pua Gardens near Kalaheo. Its name means "floral serenity," and careful attention has been given to maintaining the peaceful but exotic splendor that is so much a part of this traditional Hawaiian estate.

Originally the Manager's Estate for the Kauai Pineapple Plantation, it was founded in 1929. Seeking superior species of pineapple from around the world, the plantation staff brought back thousands of plants from their travels through the years. When pineapple cultivation ceased on Kauai, the estate was privately purchased, and although the family graciously keeps the garden open to the public, none of the buildings is accessible.

Winding paths were made for strolling through the Kau Kau Garden—a collection of food, medicinal and useful plants such as cinnamon, cocoa, coffee, banana and herbs; the "Jungle" Garden with exotics, orchids, anthuriums, heliconia, and gingers; the Palm Garden; the Hybrid Hibiscus Garden; and the Front Lawn, with its majestic shade and flowering trees.

Olu Pua Garden—a colorful oasis of rare plants and flowers with brilliant blooms every day of the year—is open Monday, Wednesday and Friday with guided tours by reservation only. Call ahead for information.

Wailua means "sacred water" and names the slowly drifting river that is the center of Kauai's most sacred and historical area. Here is an ancient "house of sanctuary," where, should they reach it in time, Hawaiians who had broken tabus could be forgiven. Nearby is Holo Holo Ku, one of the oldest **heiau** (temple) on the island. It is where human sacrifices to **Ku,** eater of men, the war god were made; and it is the site of the royal

*Hula Kahiko*

*Plumeria Lei Po'o*

*Lei papahi*

*Lei po'o*

## Water Lilies

*NYMPHAEA RUBRA*
*Pacific Tropical Botanical Garden*

→

*VICTORIA AMAZONICA*
*Pacific Tropical Botanical Garden*

*birthstone where **alii** (ruling chiefs) came to bear their children and ensure royal lineage. Caves in the riverside cliffs were secret burial tombs for Kauai royalty.*

*Smith's Tropical Paradise, thirty acres of enchanted botanical and cultural gardens, lies in a protected cove along the sacred river. Strolling paths and a narrated tram ride visit a dozen different "gardens," from the entrance lagoon with its volcano fountain to a bamboo rainforest.*

*The Japanese isle is complete with a curving red bridge and shrine. There is a Filipino village near the Fruit Basket garden with its mangos, figs, papaya, breadfruit, mulberries, milk apple, coconuts, jack fruit, soursop, guava and passion fruit, and a "wine" tree and "dill pickle" tree on either side.*

*The Traveler's Palm always grows east to west and can give directions as well as providing a quart of drinkable water. Magenta and vermillion bougainvillea splash the edges of the lily pond and duck lagoon. Lavender and purple **hono hono** orchids hang in great clumps from many trees. Hybrid hibiscus bloom in brilliant orange, red and yellow, and colors in the Flower Wheel change by season.*

*The garden's collection of Tahitian chickens, mallards, swans and mandarin ducks often stroll with visitors.*

*Adjacent to the Wailua River Boat Marina, Smith's Tropical Paradise is open daily. For guided tours, call for reservations.*

*Kauai is a feast for the eyes, lasting from dawn until dusk, and although the menu may change with the seasons, the buffet of floral beauty never grows empty.*

# Hong Kong Orchid Tree

*BAUHINIA BLAKEANA*
*Olo Pua Gardens*

# Tumeric

*CURCUMA ELATA*
*Pacific Tropical Botanical Garden*

## *Grass Palm*
CORDYLINE INDIVISA
*Olo Pua Gardens*

←

## *Areca Palm*
ARECA VESTIARIA
*Pacific Tropical Botanical Garden*

# *Red Aloe*

*ALOE SP.*
*Plantation Gardens*

→

*Plantation Gardens*
*Poipu*

# Kahili Flower

*GREVILLEA BANKSII*
*Kilauea*

# Traveler's Palm

*RAVENALA MADAGASCARIENSIS*
*Olo Pua Gardens*

*(On the following page)*

# *Torch Ginger*

*NICOLAIA ELATIOR*
*Pacific Tropical Botanical Garden*

←

*Smith's Tropical Plantation*
*Wailua*

## *Fijian Palm*

*PRITCHARDIA THURSTONII*
*Pacific Tropical Botanical Garden*

→

## *Fan Palm*

*LIVISTONA SP.*
*Smith's Tropical Plantation*

*Allerton Gardens*
*Poipu*

*THUNBERGIA MYSORENSIS*
*Pacific Tropical Botanical Garden*

# Jade Vine

*STRONGYLODON MACROBOTRYS*
*Pacific Tropical Botanical Garden*

# *Orchid*

RENANSTYLIS "QUEEN EMMA"
*Pacific Tropical Botanical Garden*

# *Erythrina*

*E. PALLIDA*
*Pacific Tropical Botanical Garden*

# *Ti*

*CORDYLINE TERMINALIS CV.*
*Pacific Tropical Botanical Garden*

*(On the following page)*

# Queen Emma Lily

*CRINUM AUGUSTUM*
*Sheraton Princeville*

# Red Passion Flower

*PASSIFLORA VITIFOLIA*
*Kokee*

# Passion Flower

*PASSIFLORA EDULIS FLAVICARPA*
*Kokee*

# Glory Bush

*TIBOUCHINA SEMIDECANDRA*
*Kokee*

*(On the following page)*

# GARDENS
# OF
# OAHU

*Aina mala pua anuenue*
*LAND WHERE RAINBOWS BLOSSOM*

*Oahu is the second oldest of the main Hawaiian Islands and perhaps the most truly beautiful of all. Two striking mountain ranges frame a verdant interior of cane fields, pineapple plantations and small, charming towns.*

*From Makapuu Point to Kahuku, the Koolaus hang from their cloud proscenium in brilliant green velvet folds, sparkling with morning rain and arched by Oahu's frequent double rainbows.*

*From Haleiwa to Pearl Harbor, the broad fertile valley-plateau is watched over by the brooding hazy-blue Waianae mountains where misty rains sweep into the valley.*

*The mountains are all that is left of two vast volcanoes from about 2.7 million years ago. Only the two inner rims of the craters remain, the outer rims lost to wind and waves millennia ago.*

*Now, all Oahu is encircled by a golden chain of coastal beach strung with pure aquamarine bays.*

*Nevermind that Honolulu is the eleventh largest city in the United States, it is still the garden it was 50 years ago.*

*Night-blooming cereus from the early 1900s still flourish along the old stone wall at Punahou School and on the slopes of Punchbowl, opening their white and gold perianths to glow palely in the hours between 8:00 p.m. and sunrise, June through October.*

*Hedges of cerise, pink and white oleander, many six and seven feet tall, nod their heavy blossoms along Kalanianaole Highway and the freeway, and pink Tecoma trees line Manoa Road.*

*Testimony to the love Hawaiians, and more recent arrivals, have for flowers is highly visible in the exquisite and educaional, public botanic gardens that ring the island.*

*In the busy center of Honolulu between freeways and city canyons of steel and glass is a cool island of green grass, stately trees and exotic orchids—**Foster Botanic Garden.***

*The story begins in 1851 with Dr. William Hillebrand who arrived in the Hawaiian Islands to marry, bought four-and-*

*a-half acres—which is now Foster Gardens—from Queen Kalama, built a modest cottage, and began collecting plants from everywhere. Some were from his own travels, some, at the urging of Kamehameha III, from obliging sea captains. In 1854 he listed 165 species of plants, including trees of great potential worth.*

*Then, in 1867, he sold his garden to Captain and Mrs. Thomas Foster and returned to Germany. The Fosters developed the garden around a lovely home, adding full-scale landscaping and an irrigation system. At Mary Foster's death in 1930, the property was bequeathed to the City of Honolulu to be maintained as a public park.*

*Under the supervision of former director Dr. Harold L. Lyon, and current director Paul R. Weissich, Foster Garden has been expanded to over twenty acres with more than 4,000 species of orchids, palms, ferns, bromeliads, gingers, ixora, spice and coffee trees. The stately big trees in the garden center are those brought to Hawaii by Dr. Hillebrand—New Zealand kauri, queen flower tree, Mindanao gum false olive and the baobab, the upside-down tree.*

*Visitors who look closely at the grass between the bromeliad plantings will find the remains of the old lava stone road.*

*For more than a century, citizens of Hawaii seemed intent on bringing to their shores all of the strange, beautiful and exotic flowers and trees of the entire tropical world.*

*Unfortunately, many varieties of plants, native to Hawaii have been lost forever. The Hawaiian Islands have the greatest number of rare and endangered species in the world, mainly because their isolated and fragile environment has been so radically changed and overdeveloped.*

*Tucked under the verdant folds of the Koolaus near Kaneohe is the newest of the city's tropical botanic gardens. **Ho'omaluhia** (peaceful refuge) opened in 1982. Here, Paul R. Weissich, director of Honolulu Botanical Gardens, has placed special emphasis on preserving and increasing the plants native and unique to Hawaii.*

*A bouquet for
Queen Liliuokalani*

*Kamehameha Parade riders*

*Little girls in plumeria leis*

*Leis for Father Damien*

This 400-acre botanic garden and nature conservancy was designed and built by the U.S. Army Corps of Engineers to provide flood protection for the area and facilities for campgrounds, hiking and a community center with classrooms and exhibition halls.

In the Kahua Koa, native plants on display include **koa** trees, Hawaii's giants of the forest; **ohia lehua; hala** or pandanus; **akia;** white hibiscus; **papala kepau; loulu** or fan palm; **palaa,** the lace fern; and **aalii.**

The adjoining Kahua Kukui contains Polynesian-introduced plants brought to Hawaii between A.D. 300 and 1200 in voyaging canoes. Among these are taro, **ti ohia ai** or mountain apple, sweet potato, banana, **hau,** kukui nut, **wauke** or paper mulberry, and **ulu** or breadfruit. Kahua Hau is dedicated to collections of **hau** from all the Pacific Islands, Japan and South Africa.

Other gardens preserve and protect plants from tropical America, India, Sri Lanka, and the magnificent and exotic trees of Africa.

A large reservoir in the center of the park is a focal point for walking trails. The gardens may all be entered from the access road, which has many parking areas. Ho'omaluhia is open daily.

On Oahu's north shore above beautiful Waimea Bay, **Waimea Falls Park,** a Hawaiian-themed garden enclave of 200 acres, was opened in 1960 as a recreation area for walking, or horse-drawn coaches.

In 1970, under the Waimea Corporation, recreation was enhanced with Hawaiian music and dancing, high dives from Waimea Falls, swans on a lily pond and a narrated tram ride through Hawaiian historical sites. The Waimea Arboretum and Botanical Garden were also opened.

Here, in the narrow, charming valley are twenty or more gardens to visit: Ogasawara Island Flora, Guam Flora, Hawaii Ethnobotanic—plants that serve man, including ones used to eat, make cloth, thatch roofs, and make medications.

*Ho'omaluhia, Kaneohe*

The Hibiscus Evolution Garden starts with Hawaii's state flower, the simple red hibiscus, and adds hundreds of single and double kaleidoscopic hybrids. One is considered a prototype of the "first ever" hibiscus.

Regarded as among the world's largest collections are pepperomia gardens, plants that produce pepper and **awa,** the lip-numbing, but non-addictive, Polynesian "welcome" drink; coral tree gardens, known in Hawaii as **wiliwili;** and Flora Malesia gardens.

There is a very complete garden of endemic Hawaiian flora. One of the prettiest and most fragrant is the lei garden—a major collection of blossoms and greenery used in Hawaiian lei-making; and the most colorful garden is Arboretum Director Keith Woolliams' collection of ginger and heliconias.

Waimea Falls Park is open daily from 10:00 a.m., some evening events, and once a month for "Moonlight Walks."

**Paradise Park** opened in 1968 in the cool reaches of Manoa Valley. Paradise Park Foundation's plan was to keep eighty percent of the park in natural foliage, and through the years to add every special rainforest flower and tree growing in the mountains of the Hawaiian Islands.

Fifteen acres of Hawaiian forest, dramatic flowers, multi-ethnic gardens, 100-year-old bamboo forests and a child-pleasing tangled maze of **hau** jungles are tucked far back in Manoa against the flanks of Mt. Olympus, where Lono, god of clouds, brings his benediction of rain.

The Hawaiian Garden contains a garden of native medicinal herbs, a food preparation house with an underground **imu,** and a host house. Here grow taro and squash and gourds and bananas and a resident flock of **nene** geese, Hawaii's endangered state bird.

On all sides are more than 100 species of plants and flowers—azalea, African tulip, magnolia, ginger in its full panoply of colors and forms, endemic and hybrid hibiscus, and heliconia.

Orchids include delicate oncidiums, hybrid vandas and showy cattleyas. There are dozens of bizarre bromeliads and *their relative, the pineapple.*

*As bright as flowers themselves are the flock of bright pink, curved-neck flamingos, standing, asleep on one long, stick-like leg or clustered together head-to-head, as if in serious conversation.*

*The jungle path through the hau is startling. A relative of hibiscus, it grows to 18 feet or more, its trunk and branches snaking along the ground and rising again to make a complex, interwoven, tangled network.*

*Iris and water lilies grace the Kings Pond, named probably for royalty who lived in the area. Both Queen Kaahumanu, one of the first queens of all Hawaii, and Queen Liliuokalani had homes in upper Manoa—Valley of Rainbows.*

*Paradise Park, open daily from 10:00 a.m., also has a Dancing Waters fountain and aviaries of exotic tropical birds that double as showmen in special entertainment.*

*A renowned botanist, on a Honolulu stopover in 1897, recommended establishing a garden running from sea level to the top of the Koolau Mountains. His suggestion was not pursued by Honolulu founders.*

*But it was a concept the Hawaiians had used for a thousand years. They knew that higher elevations are cooler and the windward side wetter. Their land management was based on the **ahupua'a**—a strip of land from the sea to the mountaintop. It provided ocean products, and the coconuts, breadfruit and taro of the coastal plains. The high forest was their source of medicinal herbs, canoe timber and fibers and feathers for their **akua** and feather cloaks.*

*The **ahupua'a** is also the concept behind the **Harold L. Lyon Arboretum,** which rises from the floor of Manoa Valley directly into the arms of the Koolaus.*

*Although a "plant testing ground," Lyon Arboretum has a close, warm feeling of "gardens are for people, plants are for people." But the arboretum is more than just plants. The oneness with the surrounding mountains is a far cry from most city-enclosed botanical gardens. This is an arboretum, and a*

*magnificent one, that opens on to another world—a wild frontier of steep ridges and narrow valleys.*

*The entrance walk from Manoa Road winds up past Hawaiian hibiscus, breadfruit and calabash trees, and a taro patch, to the Hawaiian Ethnobotanical Garden. Beyond are spathephyllum and anthurium, and gingers and heliconias as brilliant as a harbor sunset. Just before Inspiration Point is Fern Valley and the almost alien garden of bromeliads. Successive elevations from 350 to 1,600 feet provide visitors with fascinating vistas and examples of varying microclimates.*

*From Inspiration Point the view flows from the blue-green ocean up the hillsides to the top of the rugged **pali,** with Honolulu spread out below, looking like one vast garden all perfumed by mock orange, ylangylang, heliotrope and white and yellow ginger.*

*The quiet of the area, the threads of mist flowing down the mountain ravines, the vivid blooms and the twittering birds that fly busily around on their errands are reminiscent of the flowering fields on the road to Oz. Memories are made of this.*

*The Hawaii Sugar Planters Association established an experiment station here in 1918 to demonstrate the restoration of rainforests and collect plants of economic value. Its director was Dr. Harold L. Lyon, after whom the present facility is named.*

*In 1953, the arboretum became an organized research unit of the University of Hawaii at Manoa. It contains 8,500 plant varieties of some 4,000 species on 124 acres, 10 of which are open to the public. Dr. Yoneo Sagawa is director of the hillside gardens, where the cool temperatures with alternating sunshine and mist-like rains are hospitable to a magnificent display of tree ferns, ficus, philodendrons, dieffenbachia, bamboo, palms, conifers and kukui trees.*

*The gardens of Oahu may tomorrow serve people in more vital ways not yet fully understood. In the meantime, they educate, provide jobs, preserve green space, refresh the spirit and soothe the soul. They are resources of infinite value.*

# White Bird of Paradise
STRELITZIA NICOLAI
*Ho'omaluhia*

## Red Bottle Brush

*CALLISTEMON PACHYPHYLLUS*
*Ho'omaluhia*

—

## Natal Cycad

*ENCEPHALARTOS NATALENSIS*
*Ho'omaluhia*

RIEDELIA SP.
*Lyon Arboretum*

*"Jungle King" Ginger*
*ALPINA PURPURATA*
*Lyon Arboretum*

# *Erythrina*

*ERYTHRINA SPECIOSA*
*Waimea Falls Park*

47

*WAGATEA SPICATA*
*Lyon Arboretum*

# Cycad

*DIOON SPINULOSUM*
*Foster Botanical Garden*
(On the following page)

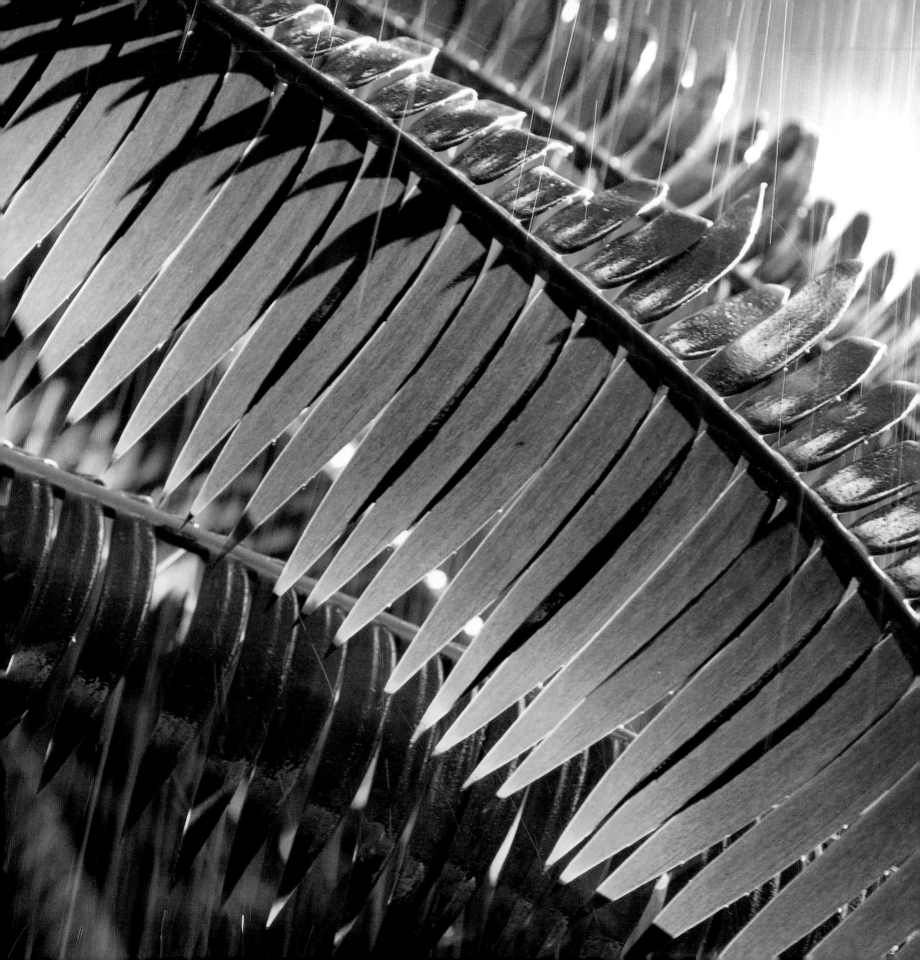

# Variegated Shell Ginger

*ALPINIA ZERUMBET*
*Waimea Falls Park*

*PANDANUS SP.*
*Waimea Falls Park*

# *"Swiss Cheese" Monstera*

*MONSTERA SP.*
*Lyon Arboretum*

# *Windows*

CALATHEA LIBBYANA
*Lyon Arboretum*

*AGAVE EGGERSIANA*
*Waimea Falls Park*

→

# Century Plant

*AGAVE SP.*
*Kailua*

# Bromeliad

*VRIESEA SP.*
*Lyon Arboretum*

# Bromeliad

*GUZMANIIA LINGULATA*
*Hart and Tagami Gallery*

# "Howard's Blue" Bromeliad

*AECHMEA HYBRID*
*Lyon Arboretum*

# Plumeria

P. RUBRA CV.
*Kaneohe*

# *Water Lily*

*NYMPHAEA SP.*
*Hart & Tagami Gallery*

# Hibiscus

CV. GRACE GOO
CV. MYELLA
HYBRID
HYBRID
Waimea Falls Park

←

# Elephant Ear

ALOCASIA SP.
Waimea Falls Park

# Orchid

HYBRID
*Foster Botanic Garden*

BRASSOCATTLEYA CLIFFTONIA MAGNIFICA
*Foster Botanic Garden*

→

*Foster Botanic Garden*
*Honolulu*

# *Kinabalu*

MEDINELLA SP.
*Lyon Arboretum*

→

*Paradise Park
Honolulu*

# Croton

*CODIAEIUM VARIEGATUM*
*Paradise Park*

*Lyon Arboretum*
*Honolulu*

# GARDENS
# OF
# MAUI

*Aina pulama ohana*
*LAND THAT EMBRACES EVERYONE*

*In an all-around poll for island popularity, Maui would probably come out the winner, which may account for its contention over the years that* **Maui no ka oi,** *"Maui is the best."*

*The broad, welcoming central valley is cradled by two great dormant volcanoes, the West Maui Mountains, and the magnificent, easily viewed, immense crater called Haleakala, "House of the Sun."*

*The Aloha State's most popular resort destination is this green and gold island the demigod Maui fished from the bottom of the ocean.*

*Maui is considerably younger than her sister islands to the northwest. The West Maui Mountains are about 1.3 million years old and Haleakala about 0.8 million years.*

*Tranquil Kealaikahiki Channel departs the western beaches of Maui and passes south between the islands of Lanai and Kahoolawe. Literally translated as "road from Tahiti," the channel is thought to have been the main ocean thoroughfare used by Polynesians as they journeyed from the Society Islands to their new home from A.D. 300 to 500. This gave Maui an early start as an ancient Hawaiian stronghold.*

*They are still arriving. More than three million people visited the "Valley Isle" last year. And the same gentle climate that brings more people yearly is just as enticing to flowers and plants from around the world.*

***Maui's Tropical Plantation,*** *just four years old, is the island's number one attraction, where visitors are taken on a "field" trip to see that things are growing great.*

*A thirty-minute, fully narrated tram tour winds through ten acres of the sometimes misty Waikapu Valley, to view coffee bushes with bright red berries and sweet white flowers on the same branch, slender papaya trees whose delicious fruit grows straight out of the trunk, sugar cane taller than the tram cars, growing pineapples, and the banana's startling blossom.*

*There's ginger—the spicy root kind—avocado, mango, guava trees and macadamia trees. The tram makes stops for photographs and sampling the fruit.*

*The heavenly scented Tropical Nursery is a veritable rainbow. There are delicate to voluptuous orchids, fiery anthuriums, double-hibiscus, heliconia and Maui's own protea. Every day is lei day at the nursery—fresh flower leis of plumeria, tuberose, Maui carnation and* **pikake** *are on display.*

*Upcountry Maui, on the slopes of Haleakala, is a different world. The drive starts with fields of gently rustling sugar cane, dry pasture land and a cactus or two. Then, at the mistline, the world turns a startling green, as green as the hills of Killarney. There are big trees and tiny villages with historic churches, great open pastures of thoroughbred horses and sleek cattle.*

*Then the flower fields appear and their fragrance mingles with a rich earth smell. In upper Kula, around every other curve on the Kula Highway or the Haleakala Highway, are fields of fragrant Maui carnations, snapdragons, gladiolus, stars of David, African daisies, lilies and, of course, protea—pink and white and red and yellow and orange, shimmering and glowing, the flower that makes people ask—"is it real?"*

*It's real, and it's named for the sea god Proteus, who could readily change into any form he chose.*

*Flowers range from delicate one-inch blossoms to a foot in diameter, from ground creepers to towering trees, and they thrive in Kula's cool mists and volcanic soil.*

*Horticulturist Dr. Philip E. Parvin, who has nurtured the Protea Research program at the University of Hawaii's Research Center in Kula, importing and crossbreeding hundreds of species from South Africa and Australia, is probably best prepared to describe some of these exotics.*

*"The King is the largest with tall, clear pink, crown-like bracts opening to a diameter of eight to twelve inches surrounding dove-gray flowers in the center. The Queen is a real showoff, about eight inches in diameter with fluffy white interior flowers, a dark crown, and fur-tipped pink bracts.*

*"The Prince and Princess, popular in England, have deep pink to coral bracts opening to gray or white flowers—how-*

# *Silversword*

*ARGYROXIPHIUM SANDWICENSE*
*Haleakala*

ever, the Prince has aristocratic straight bracts, while the Princess' bracts are curved and tipped with white lashes.

"The Duchess is a shimmering beauty of rose pink with a center of royal burgundy. The Minks share the fur-tipped bracts with the Queen and Princess—dark, lustrous mink-like fur with bracts varying from white to red.

"And the crown jewels are the Sunburst proteas—popularly known as 'pincushions.' Like a burst of fireworks in the sky, they vary from pink and yellow through orange and red. Pink Star and Hawaii Gold are among the most popular."

**Kula Botanical Gardens,** along Route 377 above Kula, has a section of protea blossoming in an incredible variety of colors.

The garden has been developed in a natural setting of two streambeds on the slopes of Haleakala. It presents an easy walk on paths surrounded by tropical and local Hawaiian plants of all varieties. The paths cross a covered bridge and wind through several arbors that offer shade and resting places. A stream accompanies one of the paths as it flows gently over several falls on its way to a pond below the reception center. From the reception center and top viewpoints in the garden, the vista of the valley, West Maui Mountains, Maalaea and Kahului bays, and the distant islands of Lanai and Molokai boggles the mind.

Warren and Helen McCord opened Kula Botanical in 1971, after they had fallen in love with Hawaii and decided they wanted to create a garden for "everyone to enjoy."

Many of their first plants came from neighbors—night-blooming cereus, fuchsias, white bird-of-paradise, and recently a calabash tree.

The proteas bloom in January through March, gingers in April through June, the flowering trees in June and July, the orchids in fall, and in December the poinsettias.

Unusual plantings for Hawaii are the ginko tree, mountain lilac, daffodils and narcissus, India wax plants and Tahitian jade.

The garden is open daily from 9:00 a.m. to 4:00 p.m.

**Sunrise Protea Farm** is a bright puddle of color, spreading over the hillside just above the Haleakala Highway turnoff to 378. There are more than 1,400 varieties of protea in the family —some three dozen thrive in the cool climate of Kula. Visitors can walk among the exotic flowers and photograph what they please of the multicolored hillsides at this 4,000-foot elevation.

The garden is open daily from 7:30 a.m. to 5:00 p.m. to view the King and Queen, Duke and Duchess, or simply opt for the brightly colored and friendly pincushions.

Just off Kula Highway before Kimo Drive are the eight acres of the **Maui Enchanting Gardens,** a relative of the Nani Mau Gardens in Hilo, Hawaii, except much younger. Where Hilo's warm humid climate produces happy exotics, Kula's misty climate is more suited to those blooms reminiscent of the mainland or England.

Look for giant-sized snapdragons and gladiolus, double carnations, glowing amaranth, statis, strawflowers, lobelia and chrysanthemums as brightly hued as a Kentucky patchwork quilt.

There is also an herb and spice garden and a colorful section of orchids, ginger and protea brushed with the colors of **anuenue,** the rainbow of Haleakala. The gardens are open daily from 9:00 a.m. to 5:00 p.m.

Rumor has it that Hana residents don't want their infamous road changed. If people could zip along at 55 miles per hour, wouldn't they miss all the breathtaking beauty? No way will the "road of 600 turns" allow more than a "slow and steady" drive through the rainforest!

The road coils along the lava, sea-buffeted coast, clinging to high cliffs, dashing down into valleys past white waterfalls and crossing 54 lichen-covered one-way bridges; all the while meandering through sword ferns, **lau hala,** kukui, **koa keawe, hou** and the rare rainbow trees. The whole area smells deliciously of ginger, plumeria, ripe guava, papaya, bananas and eucalyptus.

Along this peaceful coast is found the last of old-time

*Orchid Field, Wailuku*

*Christmas wayside shrine*

*Lei tree in Hana*

*Amaryllis*

*Carnation Farm*

Hawaii. Side roads lead to settlements time forgot. Keanae Peninsula is still a weathered enclave of taro plots. Wailua slumbers within its green fields, wooden cottages with galvanized tin roofs and yards filled with orchids, gold and green crotons and birds-of-paradise.

The nearby Miracle of Fatima Shrine, decorated for holidays and draped daily with leis, commemorates the great storm that tore beautiful white coral from the sea, leaving it at the edge of the bay to provide building material for the church.

Hana itself is a town of flowers and site of Hawaii's loveliest small hotel. It is the adopted home of the glowing brilliance of the hybrid heliconia—parrot-colored, bronze, sexy pink, royal red, orange, gold and chartreuse, with its friends the great red and pink gingers and complementary foliage—purpuria, red and green ti, rostrata and Chinese bamboo.

The somewhat spectacular arrangements in rooms of the Hana Maui Hotel owe their eye-catching enchantment to the plethora of local flowers.

In 1975, Howard Cooper opened part of **Helani Gardens,** his 70-acre commercial garden supplying the world with Hana's beauties, to share his lush and fragrant tropicals with visitors.

Among the first to bring heliconia from Costa Rica, he has gardens with more colors and varieties than he can name offhand. Waxy pink Tahitian ginger is one of his imports, and the "Helani tulip," a deep mahogany-red etlingeria ginger from India.

Helani Gardens entrance, a mass of orange trumpet vines, sparkles in the sunlight. The lower garden has five acres and 300 varieties of flowering and ornamental shrubs, trees, vines, palms, streams, bridges and pools of colorful **koi.** There are ferns and ginger, golden bamboo and weeping fig, bombax and petrea.

The upper gardens, with arbors of jade vine, fruit trees, decorative taro, shrimp plants and alacasia, extend into the 65 acres of nursery plants. The gardens are open daily from

Road to Kipahulu

9:00 a.m. to 4:30 p.m.

Beyond Hana, under the arches of the royal poinciana trees on the way to Kipahulu and the Seven Pools, roadside leimakers still hang their perfumed wares to sway from the lower branches, creating a modern kinetic advertising.

Maui's gardens do not believe that the present is only the sum of the past. While maintaining a deep purpose to protect and save the endemic and indigenous flora of the Islands, they have a blithe and exciting dedication to experimentation and innovation. What flowers were yesterday is not enough. The gardens of Maui are on their way to tomorrow's dreamed of **pua nani.**

# *Heliconia*

*H. PSITTACORUM*
*Hana*

*Wailua Falls*
*Hana Coast*

# *Heliconia*

*HELICONIA CARIBEA PURPUREA*
*Helani Gardens*

# *"Creme"*

*HELICONIA CARIBAEA*
*Olopawa Farm*

→

# *"Flash"*

*HELICONIA PURPUREA*
*Helani Gardens*

*"Sexy Pink"*
HELICONIA CHARTACEA
*Olopawa Farm*

*Pink Ginger*

NICOLAI ELATIOR
*Olopawa Farm*

## *Ornamental Banana*

MUSA VELUTINA
*Olopawa Farm*

←

## *Hala*

PANDANUS ODORATISSIMUS
*Hana Coast*

## *Water Lily*

NYMPHAEA RUBRA
*Helani Gardens*

*(On the following page)*

# Orange Trumpet Vine

*PYROSTEGIA IGNEA*
*Helani Gardens*

# Banana Flower

MUSA SP.
Maui Tropical Plantation

←

# *Jacaranda*

JACARANDA ACUTIFOLIA
*Kula*

# Candle Bush

*CASSIA ALATA*
*Maui Tropical Plantation*

# Kuhio Vine

*IPOMOEA HORSFALLIAE*
*Maui Tropical Plantation*

*Maui Tropical Plantation*
*Wailuku*

*Maui Enchanting Gardens*
*Kula*

## *Straw Flower*

*HELICHRYSUM*
*Maui Enchanting Gardens*

## *Poinsettia*

*EUPHORBIA PULCHERRIMA*
*Kula*

*(On the following page)*

# *Air Plant*

*BRYOPHYLLUM PINNATUM*
*Kula Botanical Garden*

# Fuzzy Pincushion Protea

*LEUCOSPERMUM CORDIFOLIUM*
*Maui Research Station*

*Pink Mink*

PROTEA NERIIFOLIA
*Kula*

**The Duchess**

PROTEA EXIMA
*Kula*

# Protea

GOLDEN BAKSIA
*Sunrise Protea*

RED BANKSIA
*Sunrise Protea*

# GARDENS
# OF THE
# BIG ISLAND

*Aina aloha nui ia a Pele*
*LAND BELOVED OF PELE*

The southernmost point of the United States is the still-unfinished island of Hawaii, better known as the Big Island. Its 4,038 square miles created the nickname.

So much bigger than its siblings that if Mauna Loa were lopped off at the 6,000-foot level, the whole island of Oahu would fit nicely inside.

The youngest land in the world, the Big Island's oldest mountain, Kohala, is a mere million years old. Mauna Kea is about 0.6 million, Mauna Loa less than 0.5, Hualalai less than 0.4 million, and Kilauea a hundred thousand years and growing.

So new, and with mountains so tall, not only does Hawaii have a snow ski season, but it divides into five climate sections. Hilo and the slopes of Kilauea on the northeast coast are the wettest areas and the "home of flowers." However, the northwest corner, the Kohala Coast is a place of posh hotels where exquisite gardens and golf courses have been carved from lava fields.

There is a mystique about this island. It seems closest to the ancient Hawaiian seat of power—**mana**—the phenomenal powers of Pele, goddess of volcanoes; the strength of ancient voyagers, the force of Kamehameha the Great. Should that spirit be portrayed in colors, it would be in the wild flame and scarlet and orange of anthuriums, the pulsating pinks and purples of orchids, the dark red of cooling lava in Kamuela roses, the young fires in the red-pink of Pele's **lehua**—the first tree to grow on her lava beds—and the red and orange of her own **ohelo** berries.

Hilo curves around a crescent-shaped bay on the tropical east coast and also curves around **Liliuokalani Park.** Thirty acres of delightful Japanese Edo-style gardens with tidal pools, arranged lava rocks, stone lanterns, pagodas and curved bridges plus banyans planted by famous visitors are named after Hawaii's last Queen.

Inundated twice by tidal waves, in 1946 and 1960, the garden has returned to greater beauty, although each time little was left but the banyan trees and a few stone lanterns.

In 1968, the 100th anniversary of the first arrival of Japanese immigrants, Japan presented thirteen great new stone lanterns, the wooden Torii (gateway) and the handsome stone lions guarding the entrance. Charming curved bridges were replaced, pine trees resculpted, and the aesthetic mingling of water, park, and art was reborn.

**Hawaii Tropical Botanical Garden** could be a south seas scene for a movie. Once a part of the Hamakua Coast Highway, when the road was straightened, this lovely curve was simply and appropriately named Scenic Drive.

This exquisite preserve is located seven miles north of Hilo, in seventeen acres of rainforest along the four-mile Onomea Bay coast, with a mile of woods and dell walks and 1,200 varieties of tropical plants and trees.

In 1978, Daniel Lutkenhouse sold his California business and moved to the Big Island to purchase a piece of beachside rainforest and "preserve the natural beauty of an area unequaled in any of the islands." Nearly ten years later, the botanical garden is "almost complete," and certainly more beautiful and extensive.

This garden beside Onomea Bay offers a walk through a glen of tree ferns that cast a pale green light over the path, the tiny white orchids, impatiens and unfolding fiddleheads of baby ferns. A stream dashing from Mauna Kea's slopes drops in three waterfalls, splashing immense ape plants, monstera and scarlet and green ti. A large pond is home to lavender and pink water lilies and the swiftly flickering reds and golds of prize **koi.**

Many of the plants, giant mangos, guavas, huge Alexander palms, breadfruit, kukui nut and banana trees were left as they had always grown. Dozens of new palms have been added with other lush and towering vegetation.

There are 41 kinds of ginger, 16 species of anthurium, 94 bromeliad families and 26 different types of heliconia. From time to time, breathtaking vistas of the ocean show giant

*Ama'u Fern, Kilauea*

← *Coco Palms, Kohala*

*Oyster Plant, Kailua-Kona*

Fountain Grass, Kohala

Ti at Kailua-Kona church

Kona Coffee, Kona

Ohia Lehua, Volcano

sea turtles at home in sheltered coves. The huge banyans are so old that 19th century bottles (a collector's dream) bristle from several, all securely surrounded by burgeoning trunks and roots.

A tiny former church near the entrance has been turned into a visitor's center and museum with parking in the old churchyard. Visitors are bused to the garden to roam through the seven acres.

Hawaii Tropical Botanical Garden is a private nature preserve, created to protect the harmony of a natural, tropical Hawaiian rainforest. It offers an unusual chance to see forest and shore birds that find refuge there. The garden is open daily from 9:00 a.m. to 5:00 p.m. except holidays.

Anthuriums evoke the many moods of the Big Island. It has been said they are as bold as the fiery volcanoes, as flirtatious as the goddess of fire herself and as haunting as an ocean-misted sunset.

Although they've become as indigenous as the hula, the anthuriums' early home was somewhere in tropical South America. They arrived in Hawaii about 1890.

They are at home here, where the sun warms and the rains cool. They love the mist and rain and cannot live without it. But, too much sulphur-laden rain spots the pristine waxy beauty. So their companion, the Hawaiian tree fern, protects them.

The Toyama family of **Hawaiian Flower Gardens** have grown anthuriums since 1937 in Mountain View on the slopes of Kilauea. Their "walking gardens" are still grown under tall tree ferns. Visitors like to stroll through the trees to see the glowing Toyama Red and Toyama Peach and the varicolored **obake**—the "ghost flowers"—which have strangely twisted blooms and variegated colors of green and white and pale pink. The Toyamas have added brilliant vermillion to their popular **obake.**

The Toyama Red appeared in 1937. Founder Shintaro Toyama bought three seedlings from a Mountain View front yard for a dollar each. They responded by growing into plants of beauty and joy. Their red was so new, they often took first, second and third place for red at shows because of their glowing color and perfect shape.

Under Glenn Toyama, the fifth son, the garden has also produced the "pigtail" anthurium and another "find," the Columnea Orange, for hanging baskets.

Set and hung along the walking paths are many handsome cymbidium orchids—Mrs. Tsuruko Toyama's **kuleana** (special property).

Hawaiian Flower Gardens, on South Lauko Road in Mountain View, are open daily for visitors from 9:00 a.m. to 4:00 p.m.

**Nani Mau Gardens,** about three miles south of Hilo on the highway to Volcanoes National Park, has the wonderful effect of having "just grown like Topsy," and yet the planning behind it shows, unobtrusively, in its paths, ponds and arbors. Started in 1970 by Makoto Nitahara on its present twenty acres in Panaewa, the garden began with rows of many flowering plants between rows of papaya trees in one three-acre area.

An adjacent six acres of macadamia trees were already full grown. Nitahara, his wife, and four children, converted these into an arboretum with more than 100 varieties of tropical fruit and nut trees. Fresh fruit samples of mountain apple, soursop, guava, **waiwai,** or rose apple are part of the tour.

To Nitahara, without orchids the gardens did not represent Hawaii, so three acres were landscaped with a thousand species of orchids. The next additions were a ginger garden and anthurium plantings spread under the garden's many trees.

Nani Mau became an eye-catching spread-out botanical quilt, a patchwork of sections devoted to specific types. The arbor of red jade vines is breathtaking, the breadfruit trees luxuriant, the bougainvillea riotous, and the cup of gold glows.

Nitahara has left Nani Mau Gardens to the management of his daughters and has moved on to start the very new Maui Enchanting Gardens on the slopes of Haleakala.

*Ancient hula at Hilo*

Nani Mau means "forever beautiful." And so it is.

The gardens are open daily from 8:00 a.m. to 5:00 p.m.

The Big Island is also called Orchid Isle for the 22,000 varieties that grow in and around and above the main town of Hilo.

Orchid growing started in the early 1900s as a Sunday afternoon hobby for Japanese plantation workers. Not that orchids were endemic to Hawaii. Except for two small species, they came from Java, Malaysia, South America and South Pacific islands. Perhaps the largest hothouse in the world, the Big Island is an ideal natural environment for growing orchids.

One who searched a good third of the world before settling on Hawaii as the most congenial locale for the massed blossoms of the superb and alluring Nobile dendrobium orchid is Jiro Yamamoto, founder of **Yamamoto Dendrobiums Hawaii** in 1974.

Here, at Mountain View, are three acres of greenhouses with hundreds of plants in 87 varieties and colors with as many romantic names.

Gold Grace is a clean, pure golden blossom, Pink Elegance is white with a pale yellow throat and pink-tipped petals and Tancho Princess is pure white, with the faintest dusting of yellow around a ruby-brown throat.

A sturdy plant will have as many as fifteen canes (stalks) with twenty or more flowers on each cane—a big, showy, colorful, double armful of the world's most exotic blooms.

The garden is open weekdays at the 13 Mile Marker on Volcanoes National Park Highway, through the flowering season, from 9:00 a.m. to 3:00 p.m.

**Hilo Tropical Gardens** is a two-acre flower quilt of many colors of orchids and tropical blossoms as well as shade trees and tidepools. New owner, Jean Wright, has added a whole new array of Hawaii's fragrant flowers—gardenia, **pikake**, tuberose, tiare tahiti, and plumeria to perfume the seaside garden. She's added a hula performance for Saturday morning visitors and started a ginger garden flushed with the colors of pink and red ginger, torch ginger and dainty shell ginger. The charming lady who strings leis and explains the garden really is named Aunty Aloha.

Located at 1477 Kalanianaole Avenue, just past Onekahakaha Beach and two miles from Hilo Airport, Hilo Tropical is open daily from 8:30 a.m. to 4:30 p.m.

Hawaiians say **"Ka nani o na pua i mohala"** (Behold the beauty of the blossom as it unfolds).

"As the sun rises, the flower buds tremble to start their birth. Slowly one petal opens, another moves, bumping against the first. Another opens and another which curls daintily; more petals stretch and preen. Until opened to its full beauty, the flower looks up to the sun and joyously bestows its fragrance upon the morning world."

So has **PUA NANI** opened to show its many flowers.

For all Hawaii is truly a garden.

# Ohia Lehua

METROSIDEROS COLLINA SSP. POLYMORPHA
*Kilauea*

# Fern Forest

*Hawaii Volcanoes National Park*

(On the following page)

# Ama'u Ferns

*SADLERIA CYATHEOIDES*
*Volcano*

## *Toyama Red*

ANTHURIUM ANDREANUM CV.
*Hawaii Flower Gardens*

## *Pretty Peach*

ANTHURIUM ANDREANUM CV.
*Hawaii Flower Gardens*

→

## *Obake*

ANTHURIUM ANDRAEANUM
*Hawaii Tropical Botanical Garden*

# *Bromeliad*

TILLANDSIA HELICONIOIDES
*Hawaii Tropical Botanical Garden*

# Hanging Heliconia

*HELICONIA COLLINSIANA*
*Hawaii Tropical Botanical Garden*

# Bird of Paradise
*STRELITZIA REGINAE*
*Hilo*

# Red Thai Banana

*MUSA COCCINEA*
*Hawaii Tropical Botanical Garden*

*Cup of Gold*
SOLANDRA HARTWEGI
Nani Mau Gardens

*African Tulip Tree*
SPATHODEA CAMPANULATA
Laupahoehoe

115

# Shell Ginger

*ALPINA NUTANS*
*Nani Mau Gardens*

# Pink Bombax

*PSEUDOBOMBAX ELLIPTICUM*
*Nani Mau Gardens*

# Breadfruit Tree

*ARTOCARPUS ALTILIS*
*Opihikao*

# Giant Taro

*ALOCASIA MACRORRHIZA*
*Hawaii Tropical Botanical Garden*

→

*Hawaii Tropical Botanical Garden*
*Onomea*

*Hawaii Tropical Botanical Garden*
*Onomea*

←

# Red Jade Vine

*MUCANA NOVI-GUINEENSIS*
*Nani Mau Gardens*

# *Ti*

*CORDYLINE TERMINALIS CV.*
*Hawaii Tropical Botanical Garden*

*Red Ginger*
ALPINIA PURPURATA
*Hilo*

→

**Monstera**
MONSTERA DELICIOSA
*Rainbow Falls, Hilo*

# Dendrobium

DENDROBIUM NOBILE "TANCHO PRINCESS"
Yamamoto Gardens

# Baron Sandy

*DENDROBIUM SP.*
*Hilo Tropical Gardens*

*"Nellie Morley"*
*VANDA SP. ORCHID*
*Hilo Tropical Gardens*

→

# Orchid

*PHALAENOPSIS HYBRID*
*Hilo Tropical Gardens*

# *Bougainvillea*
### BOUGAINVILLEA SPECTABILIS VAR. LATERITIA
### *Kailua-Kona*

**Pua Nani** is a book that I have wanted to do for a long time. I have been photographing flowers and plants since I first came to Hawaii. Most of this book was, however, photographed in the last year. It has been a labor of love.

Technically, almost all the photos were shot using a Pentax 6x7 camera and three lenses (45mm, 75mm, and 135mm macro). The film stock throughout the book was Fujichrome 100 with processing by Light Inc. The Fujichrome film provided incredibly beautiful color, from greens to reds, with great resolution and shadow detail. The processing was excellent with absolute consistency of color and speed.

The most important aspect of shooting flora, however, is finding good weather. Surprisingly this does not mean waiting for the sun.

The seemingly worst weather that I encountered was on a 6:00 a.m. flight to Hilo. It was raining so hard when we landed that I asked the flight attendant if I could just stay on the plane and return to Honolulu. The return flight was sold out, so I rented a car and drove out to the garden. It never cleared up completely, but it did stop raining. I was able to get a number of photos that morning including the anthurium on the cover.

Actually the perfect weather for shooting flowers and plants is partly cloudy with no wind. Too much wind is the one thing that can ruin your day. If it's too windy, about the only thing I can recommend is to go sailing. That's what I did.